Wisdom from
AFRICA

A collection of proverbs

Wisdom from
AFRICA

A collection of proverbs

Compiled by Dianne Stewart
Illustrated by Caine Swanson

I wish to thank Linda de Villiers, Cecilia Barfield and Helen Henn.
Dianne Stewart

Struik Lifestyle
(an imprint of Penguin Random
House South Africa (Pty) Ltd)
Company Reg, No. 1953/000441/07
The Estuaries, 4 Oxbow Crescent,
Century Avenue, Century City 7441
PO Box 1144, Cape Town 8000,
South Africa

First published by
Struik Publishers in 2005
Reprinted in 2006, 2007, 2008
Reprinted by Struik Lifestyle in 2010,
2011, 2013, 2014, 2016, 2019

www.penguinrandomhouse.co.za

Publisher: Linda de Villiers
Editor: Cecilia Barfield
Designer: Helen Henn
Illustrator: Caine Swanson

Reproduction:
Hirt & Carter Cape (Pty) Ltd
Printing and binding:
TWP Sdn. Bhd., Malaysia

ISBN 978-1-77007-026-4

Contents

Introduction

African proverbs have their source in the oral tradition. Traditionally, these wise sayings were passed on – by word of mouth – from one generation to the next. But in more recent times they have been recorded to preserve them for posterity.

Solomon Lysere states that the modern African writer is to his indigenous oral tradition as a snail is to its shell. Even in a foreign habitat, a snail never leaves its shell behind. The Kaonde (Zambia) proverb *Kwenda kwa kolokofwa ne nzubo yanji*, which translates as 'the journey of a snail and its house', expresses the sentiment that wherever a wise man travels, he takes his wisdom with him, like a snail that travels with its house. In the same way, the contemporary African writer is aware of his heritage contained in the communal wisdom of his people.

African proverbs reflect both the past and present, and are as relevant to contemporary society as they were to traditional society. They abound in imagery and it was the rich, vibrant and profound use of figurative language in proverbs, riddles, idioms and oral poetry that first attracted me to these genres as a student of African languages.

In order to understand the full meaning and cultural significance of an African proverb, it may be necessary to decode it, as a literal translation often fails to capture its true meaning. For example, the Gikuyu (Kenya) proverb *Mbaara ti ûcûrû*, which translates as 'War is not porridge', requires such decoding. In traditional Gikuyu society the consumption of porridge was considered a wholesome, integral part of everyday life and was even offered to guests. At a meal if any was left over, people were encouraged to eat more of it to satisfy their hunger. The Gikuyu people use this proverb to demonstrate that, unlike porridge, which is highly desirable, war is never desirable and has a devastating effect on the lives of people.

African proverbs have both practical and philosophical relevance. The Lugbara (Uganda) proverb *Amvu ni 'ba anyajo ni* with its English translation 'A man's field is his stomach', addresses a practical aspect of life, i.e. a man's fields provide food for him therefore he must cultivate them. The Sotho (Lesotho) proverb *Mohana ho jwetswa o tshohela leomeng*, translated as 'A word is sufficient for the wise', is an example of an African proverb of philosophical significance.

Most African proverbs are short and succinct, enabling hearers or readers to memorize and repeat them easily. For instance, *Taba di mahlong* (Sotho, Lesotho) is translated as 'It is the face that is the index of the mind'. They also demonstrate some universal or cultural truth that is familiar to the hearers or readers. The Soga people of Uganda have a wise saying that is universally applicable: *Amaadhi amasabe tigamala ndigho* with the translation 'When one begs for water it does not quench the thirst'. This proverb is used to encourage one to work to satisfy one's own needs rather than ask favours of other people in order to be fulfilled.

Proverbs that are used to describe human nature and human behaviour abound in the languages of the African continent. Sometimes they are used to caution people against certain forms of behaviour, at other times proverbs are used as an encouragement.

The Zulu-speaking people of KwaZulu-Natal use a strong proverb to refer to someone who is a liar or two-faced. They say *Ulimi mbili*, which translates as 'He has two tongues' and it means that at one moment he will offer one viewpoint and then quickly change his viewpoint, depending on his audience.

The Swahili proverb heard in East Africa, *Haba na haba hujaza kibaba* and translated as 'little by little the measure is filled', is offered to encourage people to persist in achieving their goals, as a task is often completed step by step.

African proverbs are used as a means of moral instruction at all levels of society. The Njak (Nigeria) proverb, *Laa mang goetok goeman muan wu soeng*, translated as 'The child who is carried on the back will not know how far the journey is', cautions parents against overprotecting their children.

The importance of respect and reverence for elders in African society is demonstrated by the Rwanda (Rwanda) and Rundi (Burundi) proverb *Ndani ya neno la mzee hupatikana mfupa*. The literal translation, 'a bone is formed from the word of an elder' when decoded further signifies that the youth should look to the elders in their society for guidance and instruction.

As the natural environment was very important to traditional African societies, one finds numerous animal and bird sayings, some of which are used to highlight aspects of the human condition. An example is the Mali proverb, *Jirikurun men on men ji la, a te ke bama ye*. The literal translation is 'a log may stay in the water for a long time, but it won't turn into a crocodile'. This saying of the wise encourages people to be true to themselves.

Another example of the role that African proverbs play in the education and instruction of members of society is found in the Wolof proverb from Senegal, *Ku la abal l tank, nga dem fa ko neex*, which is translated as 'If you borrow a man's legs you will go where he directs you.' This demonstrates that if one becomes too heavily indebted to someone, one will lose one's independence as a result.

Sometimes, the same proverb occurs in different languages in different countries, illustrating the universal nature of some of these wise sayings. Not only are they currency in private conversations but they are also used in public as a means of informing and influencing the behaviour of individuals and groups.

Dianne Stewart

Dedication
For Emeritus Professor
Ant Davey, who inspired my
studies in African Languages

wisdom

Nunya, adidoe, asi metunee o.
(Akan: Ghana)

Wisdom is like a baobab tree. One individual cannot embrace it.

Explanation:
No individual may claim to have all the wisdom there is.

Joki nô ga volo, ni baka ei gpi murtu.
(Balanda/Belanda Viri: Eritrea)

God is a great eye. He sees everything in the world.

Explanation:
As God sees all that one does, this proverb urges one to choose good rather than evil.

Mohana ho jwetswa o tshohela leomeng.
(Sotho: Lesotho)

A word is sufficient for the wise.

Explanation: People who do not want to listen to advice, often land up in trouble.

wisdom **11**

Enye enyene eti ibuut.
(Efik: Nigeria)

He has a good head.

Explanation:
He is a man of understanding.

Haba na haba hujaza kibaba.
(Swahili: East Africa)

Little by little the measure is filled.

Explanation:
Persistent effort helps to complete a task.

Takipar bich che meloljinge ma.
(Tugen: Kenya)

It is easy to defeat people who do not kindle fire for themselves.

Explanation:
Traditionally, in Tugen society, the
elders would sit around the fire and
discuss issues of concern to the
community in order to maintain
stability and unity. If the fire is
not kindled for this purpose,
or symbolically if the people
do not value and appreciate
each other, the proverb
warns that they will
easily be defeated in
a time of trial.

Ihsani (hisani) haiozi.
(Swahili: East Africa)

Kindness does not spoil.

Explanation:
Kindness lasts.

Bophelo ke molaetsa. Thee letsa.
(Northern Sotho: South Africa)

Life is a message. Heed it.

Explanation:
Learn from life's experiences.

Ukuph' ukuziphakela.
(Zulu: South Africa)

Giving is to serve a portion for oneself.

Explanation:
Kindness is reciprocated. When one gives to another it is like serving a portion for oneself because when in need, it is most likely that the person one has helped will return the kindness.

Amaadhi amasabe tigamala ndigho.
(Soga: Uganda)

When one begs for water it does not quench the thirst.

Explanation:
Often, something that one begs for is not exactly what one requires. It may be insufficient or not to one's liking. This proverb encourages one to work, to satisfy one's own needs rather than ask favours of other people.

Epuku liocili te eli lioku pukula Suku.
(Umbundu: Angola)

God's displeasure is a serious matter; one can endure the displeasure of others.

Explanation:
It is more important to fear God than man.

Aachaye kweli huirudia.
(Swahili: East Africa)

He who leaves behind truth, returns to it.

Explanation:
Someone who has done good in an area will be welcomed back when he or she returns.

Kwenda kwa kolokofwa ne nzubo yanji.
(Kaonde: Zambia)

The journey of a snail and its house.

Explanation:
Wherever a man who is
wise travels, he takes
his wisdom with him,
like a snail that
travels with
its house.

Omukiintu ontungwa.
(Ovambo: Namibia)

A woman is a basket.

Explanation:
A woman never walks around without carrying a
basket. This proverb highlights the fact that women
are resourceful.

human nature

Izandla ziyagezama.
(Zulu: South Africa)

Hands wash each other.

Explanation:
There is mutual interdependence in the act of hand-washing. Likewise, people depend on each other.

Ku la abal I tank, nga dem fa ko neex.
(Wolof: Senegal)

If you borrow a man's legs, you will go where he directs you.

Explanation:
If one is too heavily indebted to someone, one will lose one's independence.

Kukwata mulwanyi ku mubenza.
(Kaonde: Zambia)

To catch an enemy you need to stalk him.

Explanation:
One needs to be patient in order to solve a problem.

Umhaw' usuk' esweni.
(Zulu: South Africa)

Jealousy begins with the eye.

Explanation:
It is usually when one has seen something that one
becomes jealous of it.

Enyene ison-ika.
(Efik: Nigeria)

He has but one word.

Explanation:
This proverb refers to a man of integrity, a man who
always speaks the truth.

Mwenye moyo wa furaha humzaidia raha.
(Swahili: East Africa)

The person who has a cheerful heart will discover that joy is always on the increase.

Explanation:
A person who is contented finds that joy keeps
flowing into his or her life.

Ondjala yopela kay'ehama,
ondjuulukwe okamana.
(Ovambo: Namibia)

Hunger pangs are not painful: longing kills.

Explanation:
Longing has a negative effect on one. It makes one
thinner than hunger does.

Omba dra ni.
(Lugbara: Uganda)

Anger is death.

Explanation:
Anger can lead to disastrous situations. The proverb
cautions one to keep one's anger under control.

Ubukulu abubangwa.
(Xhosa: South Africa)

One does not achieve greatness by claiming greatness.

Explanation:
A man is judged by his actions, not his boasting.

Bo tsholwa bo tjhesa, bo tsohe bo fodile.
(Sotho: Lesotho)

In time, tempers cool down.

Explanation:
A heated argument eventually subsides.

Umenziw' akakhohlwa, kukhohlw' umenzi.
(Zulu: South Africa)

The person who has been offended is always mindful of it; the person who offends, forgets it.

Explanation:
The person who has been offended by someone remembers the grievance far more than the person who committed it.

Taia nohto les.
(Krio: Sierra Leone)

Tiredness is not the same as laziness.

Explanation:
If a person is not performing a task because he is tired,
it does not imply that he is lazy.

Kiaribucho urafiki ni kukopa na kuazima.
(Swahili: East Africa)

Borrowing and lending spoil a friendship.

Explanation:
Borrowing and lending can lead to disharmony
between friends or colleagues.

Jina jema hungara gizani.
(Swahili: East Africa)

A reputable name stands out even in the dark.

Explanation:
A good name is to be treasured.

Kazana kulima, vyakupewa havitoshelezi.
(Bena: Tanzania)

Persevere with farming, handouts will not satisfy you.

Explanation:
Handouts will help one in the short term, but in order to feel fulfilled, one needs to earn one's own living.

Woth' omabili.
(Zulu: South Africa)

He basks in both suns.

Explanation:
This proverb refers to an elderly person who sits in the morning and afternoon sun in order to keep warm.

Majuto hayatangulii.
(Swahili: East Africa)

Remorse is never first.

Explanation:
Remorse for a misdeed that has been committed, only comes after the event. One does not feel regret before committing the wrongdoing.

Bala gna fadhiana diaka verle.
(Wolof: Senegal, The Gambia)

Before one heals others, heal oneself.

Explanation:
One first needs to remove the beam from one's own eye before one tries to remove the speck from someone else's eye.

Uukadhona omwene.
(Ovambo: Namibia)

Girlhood has its own master.

Explanation:
A young girl is responsible for and to herself.

Muchima wa mukwenu munkundwe.
(Kaonde: Zambia)

The heart of another is a wilderness.

Explanation:
One will never know exactly what another person
is thinking or feeling.

family
life

Kahola omutoye, nakufu omutoye.
(Ovambo: Namibia)

The first fruits are sweet, but so are the autumn fruits.

Explanation:
The first child is as special to the parents as the youngest.

Ibi ti ayiye ba ba'ni, ni a ti nje.
(Yoruba: Nigeria)

Home is where life is found in all its fullness.

Explanation:
Home is the place where one feels most contented.

*Lou jalele vaja thia saine
keurre la ko deguey.*
(Wolof: Senegal, The Gambia)

What the child says, it has heard at home.

Explanation:
One should be careful of what one says in front of children as they are likely to repeat it outside the home.

Mbeleko moja haibebi watoto wawili.
(Kuria: Tanzania)

Two children cannot be held by a single cloth.

Explanation:
It is better to do one thing at a time.

Ukuzal' ukuzilungelela.
(Zulu: South Africa)

To give birth to children is to add on to oneself.

Explanation:
As children grow, parents are able to delegate some of their work to their children. In this way children are perceived as an extension of their parents.

Laa mang goetok goeman muan wu soeng.
(Njak: Nigeria)

A child who is carried on the back will not know how far the journey is.

Explanation:
A child carried on the back will not be able to gauge how far it has travelled because it has not undertaken the journey itself. This proverb is used to caution others that overprotecting a child does not encourage the child to become independent.

Jalele bagna na lo mou tamma.
(Wolof: Senegal, The Gambia)

The child hates the one who gives it all it wants.

Explanation:
Spare the rod, spoil the child.

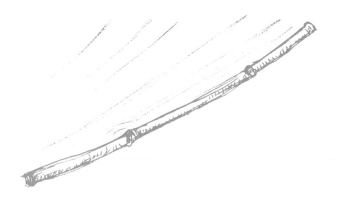

'Ba si jo yi dria ku.
(Lugbara: Uganda)

People do not build a house on top of water.

Explanation:
A home must be built on a solid foundation. This proverb may also be used to express the idea that reason needs to be the foundation of an argument.

Annaatu du-e jedhe/kan thuutho ijolle fithe.
(Oromo: Ethiopia)

'Hunger is causing me to die', said the person who had drunk the child's bottle.

Explanation:
Great need can motivate a person to do despicable things.

Ukuwa kwendlu wukuvuka kwenye.
(Zulu: South Africa)

When one house falls, another flourishes.

Explanation:
This proverb is used when a young, capable girl leaves her home and goes to another household at the time of her marriage. It signifies that one family's loss is another family's gain.

Akukho mful' ungahlokomi.
(Zulu: South Africa)

There is not a river that flows without a sound.

Explanation:
Every home has its quarrels.

Aberewa hwe abofra ma ofifir se nna abofra so hwe aberewa ma nese tutu.
(Akan: Ghana)

**The mother feeds the baby
daughter before she has teeth,
so the daughter will feed the mother
when she loses her teeth.**

Explanation:
The mother takes care of her daughter and it is hoped
that her daughter in turn will look after her mother in
her old age.

Kud mbelawa a hada a hwad.
(Mafa: Cameroon, Nigeria, Niger)

An orphan's tears run inside.

Explanation:
During difficult times orphans may be neglected by the extended family who is looking after them. Normally tears on the cheek are seen, but in this instance, tears run inside and are not seen. This proverb is used in the context of orphans or those people who detect social injustice but are powerless to do anything about it.

*Majembe yalimayo pamoja
hayakosi kugongana.*
(Swahili: East Africa)

Hoes that dig together often knock each other.

Explanation:
People who live or work together do quarrel at times.

adversity

Angu 'bu a ri yuku ani.
(Lugbara: Uganda)

The elevated place is for kites.

Explanation:

Although kites can fly high enough to fly away,
human beings cannot do the same. If they run away,
they will no doubt be found. This proverb is also used
to warn proud people who want to elevate themselves
to high positions.

Kikulacho ki nguoni mwako.
(Swahili: East Africa)

The thing that eats you, is in what you wear.

Explanation:
Trouble is often caused by those closest to one.

Uzipembela emoyeni.
(Xhosa: South Africa)

You are lighting a fire in the wind.

Explanation:
This proverb refers to a person who is kinder to
strangers than relatives, which is to his own
disadvantage as it is a dangerous way of behaving.

Wahlalwa yilahl' emhlane.
(Zulu: South Africa)

A burning coal sits on his back.

Explanation:
This proverb refers to someone who is constantly
plagued by troubles and afflictions.

'Ba dra aza ama dra 'baruri aza si.
(Lugbara: Uganda)

People understand the pain of sickness
by experiencing it themselves.

Explanation:
Someone who has never experienced pain, sickness or
suffering cannot really empathise with others who are
experiencing difficulties.

Onipa ho anto no a, na efi ne nneyee.
(Akan: Ghana)

If one is unhappy, the cause for one's unhappiness is within oneself.

Explanation:
One is often to blame for one's own unhappiness. This proverb from Ghana encouragess one to accept responsibility for one's own challenging circumstances instead of blaming others for them.

Ilizwe lifile.
(Xhosa: South Africa)

The land has died.

Explanation:
This proverb implies that war has begun.

Wo to adur-a ebi ka w'ano.
(Oji: Nigeria)

If you put down poison (i.e. attempt to poison others) some will touch your mouth.

Explanation:
Being unkind to others will have a detrimental effect on oneself as well.

Tlaila le tlailel morena.
(Sotho: Lesotho, South Africa)

Do not be afraid to make mistakes so that they can be corrected.

Explanation:
If one never made errors or mistakes, one might not discover the correct or most expedient way of doing things.

Usigonge nguzo ukasingizia giza.
(Swahili: East Africa)

Do not put the blame on the darkness if you bump into a pole.

Explanation:
If you knowingly go into a dangerous situation, do not be surprised if you get hurt.

Ba betsana ka noga e utloa.
(Tswana: Botswana)

They beat each other with a snake that is alive.

Explanation:
They are at loggerheads with each other.

Ohia na ma odece ye akoa.
(Oji: West Africa)

Poverty transforms a free man into a slave.

Explanation:
When a man becomes penniless, he does not have the freedom and options that he had when he had money.

Lefu ha le jwetse.
(Sotho: Lesotho)

Death may strike at any moment.

Explanation:
No one can escape death.

Yiz' uvalo, inqobo yisibindi.
(Zulu: South Africa)

It is not fear, but courage that is important.

Explanation:
This proverb is used to encourage someone in a difficult situation.

Onipa fa adamfo ansa na wanya amane.
(Akan: Ghana)

It is preferable for one to make friends before one encounters difficulties.

Explanation:

It is wise to make friends early so that they can come to one's aid when troubles occur. Otherwise one might have to face one's difficulties alone.

Tlala e lala tlas'a sesiu.
(Sotho: Lesotho, South Africa)

Famine sleeps under the basket used for grain.

Explanation:
Although the grain basket is full, one never knows when it may be empty. This proverb refers to the fact that one never knows what is around the corner.

Ohaa fululula iilambo iikulu.
(Ovambo: Namibia)

They are digging old holes again.

Explanation:
They are digging up old disputes, to the detriment of themselves and others.

good
fortune

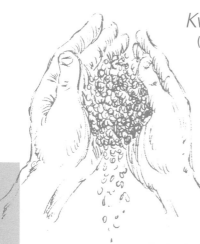

Kwa kukuta, oko ku nonkenya.
(Ovambo: Namibia)

The hard thing has a seed in it.

Explanation:
When people persevere, prosperity will follow.

Akili ni ndonge.
(Sheng: Kenya)

The use of intelligence creates wealth.

Explanation:
Clever planning leads to success that will reap
monetary rewards. The Sheng language is a short form
of Swahili and English, used by the youth of Nairobi.

Rentshana se se mo inong.
(Tswana: Botswana)

We pick each other's teeth.

Explanation:
This proverb is used to describe two people who are on
very good terms with each other.

*Kou tey jamone ndialbene, moudhie
di noflaye.*
(Wolof: Senegal, The Gambia)

If you are familiar with the beginning, the end will not give you trouble.

Explanation:
If you plan a task well at the beginning, the chances of successful completion will be greater.

Abema hamoi basindika eitara.
(Haya: Tanzania)

Many hands make light work.

Explanation:
If many people share the workload, it becomes lighter.

Tama sugo diniabe.
(Kanuri: Nigeria)

Hope is the pillar of the world.

Explanation:
Hope is a stronghold in a world of fluctuating
circumstances.

Khotso, pula, nala.
(Sotho: Lesotho)

Peace, rain, prosperity.

Explanation:
When peace and rain abound, people are contented as
they are not fighting. They are ploughing their fields
and enjoying good fortune.

Fa go chele madiba a magolo,
rona re tla bonala kae?
(Tswana: Botswana)

Now that the great lakes have become dry, what shall become of us?

Explanation:
When one door shuts, another opens.

Ongundja ihay' ende nakaanda.
(Ovambo: Namibia)

The grain owner does not carry a larder.

Explanation:
One cannot carry one's wealth around with one.

Okulonga uuwanawa ompunda
yomagadhi omatoye.
(Ovambo: Namibia)

Doing good is a honey-comb.

Explanation:
The person who is kind to others, has many friends.

community

Sisimizi hawaumani.
(Kuria: Tanzania)

A black ant will not bite another black ant.

Explanation:
People who are members of the same group should not fight against each other.

Wan han noh de tai bohndul.
(Krio: Sierra Leone)

A bundle cannot be fastened with one hand.

Explanation:
No man is
completely self-
sufficient. We
have need of
each other.

Nitte de na anda ak morome
am tey dou masse am.
(Wolof: Senegal, The Gambia)

A person should take as his companion someone who is older than himself.

Explanation:
One should take advice from someone who is older
than oneself as that person is likely to have wisdom
and experience.

'Ba alu pamvu siri (a) ru.
(Lugbara: Uganda)

The footprint (track) of only one person is narrow.

Explanation:
Unlike a single track, many travellers create a wide path. This Lugbara proverb refers to the fact that someone working on his own does not achieve as much as those who work together to achieve success.

Soba tsirebe musko ndin tei.
(Kanuri: Nigeria)

Hold a true friend with both your hands.

Explanation:
Treasure a good friend. Nurture the friendship.

Enongonongo kalu vulu okuikalela.
(Ovambo: Namibia)

A parasite cannot live on its own.

Explanation:
No person wants to live alone.

Umoja ni nguvu, utengano ni udhaifu.
(Kiha: Tanzania)

There is strength in unity, but weakness in division.

Explanation:
Unity is strength, division is weakness.

Umuzi ngumuzi ngokuphanjukelwa.
(Zulu: South Africa)

A home is a home if it is visited.

Explanation:
People will not visit a home where hospitality is not offered. This proverb encourages kindness even to strangers, so that one's home will be visited often.

Bi ille ko kan ille ki ijo ajoran.
(Yoruba: Nigeria)

Houses that are not close to each other, do not easily catch fire.

Explanation:
Familiarity breeds contempt. People who are not familiar with each other have a better relationship.

time

N'iritagira inkoko riraca.
(Kirundi: Burundi)

A night with no roosters will still end.

Explanation:
Hope does not rest only on things that are seen.

Izinsuk' amathanda kwenzelwa.
(Zulu: South Africa)

Days like to be provided for.

Explanation:
It is necessary to make provisions for the bad times.
One should also plan for the future.

Aakulu taa siluka, aape taa tumbu.
(Ovambo: Namibia)

The old go down and the young rise.

Explanation:
Time and the world moves on

Kunanga kwa kumakya
kusambakana banyama.
(Kaonde: Zambia)

In order to find animals, you need to hunt in the morning.

Explanation:
The early bird catches the worm.

Ke gu bonetse letsatsi pele.
(Tswana: Botswana)

I have seen the sun before you have.

Explanation:
I was born even before you could see. Experience has
taught me many things.

Bikondama kuya nshiku bikoloka.
(Kaonde: Zambia)

All bent things will be
straightened as days pass.

Explanation:
Time heals all wounds.

time *73*

Lepotla-potla le ja poli;
lesisitheho le ja khomo.
(Sotho: Lesotho)

The hurry-hurry person eats goat. The one who takes his time eats beef.

Explanation:
The one who does things in a hurry will not achieve the
same effect as the one who takes his time to do
the task. Patience has its rewards.

Haraka haraka haina baraka.
(Swahili: Kenya)

Hurry hurry has no benefits.

Explanation:
There is little merit in doing things in a hurry.

Uulelekule wa ndjila.
(Ovambo: Namibia)

Endless road.

Explanation:
If I had been closer [to you], I would have arrived
on time.

'Ba azi osile si be ni yo.
(Lugbara: Uganda)

No-one has teeth at birth.

Explanation:
It takes time for a project to develop, just as teeth take
time to grow in a child's mouth.

Lou nga telle telle dioka, yonne dhitou la.
(Wolof: Senegal, The Gambia)

The person who rises early in the morning, finds the journey short.

Explanation:
The person who starts a task early, finds little difficulty in completing it.

Ukugug' akumemezi.
(Zulu: South Africa)

Old age arrives unannounced.

Explanation:
Nothing marks the transition from middle to old age. It arrives suddenly.

Inkonan' ikhethwa kusakhanya.
(Zulu: South Africa)

The calf is removed from its mother when it is still light.

Explanation:
Calves are separated from their mothers at night otherwise there would be no milk left by morning. It is good to do things timeously.

A ki wo ago alago sise.
(Yoruba: Nigeria)

We do not work by another man's clock.

Explanation:
It is not in a person's best interests to imitate other
people's lifestyles or to try to be like them.

communication

Wabanjw' untsho.
(Xhosa: South Africa)

The eagle is trapped.

Explanation:
When defending oneself one can inadvertently
say something that implicates one.

Ho bua hase ho phetha.
(Sotho: Lesotho)

Great talkers are never great doers.

Explanation:
This proverb warns against those who have much to
say about a matter, but do little about it.

Msema kweli hana wajoli.
(Swahili: East Africa)

The person who speaks the truth does not have friends.

Explanation:
Bearers of the truth are often not welcomed.

*Wax soxu fetal la; su reccee,
dabu ko wees.*
(Wolof: Senegal)

Words resemble bullets; if they escape one cannot retrieve them.

Explanation:
This proverb warns one to consider carefully what one says. Words can hurt and are not easily retracted.

Abi ma bi(le) ci.
(Lugbara: Uganda)

Walls do have ears.

Explanation:
This proverb serves as a warning that someone might be overhearing one's conversation. It also may be used to refer to an individual present who is not trustworthy; therefore caution needs to be exercised.

Indlu yegag' iyanetha.
(Zulu: South Africa)

The house of a person who talks too much lets in the rain.

Explanation:
This proverb is used to describe a person who is so partial to talking that he neglects essential duties like repairing his house. Not only does his house leak, but this person will not fare well during a time of trial. His 'big talk' attitude will be revealed.

Siri ni kwa mtu mmoja.
(Swahili: East Africa)

A secret is the possession of only one person.

Explanation:
If a secret is shared, it is no longer a secret.

Namukaga gwaa li ombwa.
(Ovambo: Namibia)

A dog is not killed by eating without oil.

Explanation:
A man is not killed by gossip.

*Ella waja bou ntoute, tey
deguelou bou barey.*
(Wolof: Senegal, The Gambia)

One must talk less and listen more.

Explanation:
To listen is more valuable than to speak.

Wande ngomlomo njengesiqabetho.
(Zulu: South Africa)

He is wide mouthed like a basket.

Explanation:
This refers to a large, wide-mouthed Zulu basket and is
used to describe a person who talks incessantly but
does little.

A'i-azi pi edre okaru (kaniku dedeleru).
(Lugbara: Uganda)

The co-wives' tongue is bitter.

Explanation:
The communication between co-wives is often
characterized by bitterness and anger. The proverb is
used to warn people against communication of this
nature. On the other hand, it shows that this is normal
and that the disagreements between co-wives should
not be taken too seriously.

animals

Jirikurun men on men ji la, a te ke bama ye.
(Bambara: Mali)

A log may stay in the water for a long time, but it doesn't turn into a crocodile.

Explanation:
This proverb highlights the fact that one cannot be what one is not and it encourages one to be oneself.

*Bophokoje ba ba nkgoe ba itsanye
ka mebala.*
(Tswana: Botswana)

Grey jackals know each other
because of their speckles.

Explanation:
One is comfortable with, and seeks out, those who are
similar to oneself.

Lya ka kali nuukali na nkombwena.
(Ovambo: Namibia)

A goat that is old does not
spare a young goat.

Explanation:
A man has no empathy for a child who is not his own.

Nala kungekho qhude liyasa.
(Zulu: South Africa)

Even when the rooster (cock) is not present, day dawns.

Explanation:
Even when the rooster is not present to announce the dawn, it will still occur. This proverb is said of a person who thinks he is indispensable.

Ntja e tsokela ya e fang.
(Tswana: South Africa)

A dog will follow the one who feeds it.

Explanation:
People will respond favourably to those who are kind
to them.

Wapiganapo tembo nyasi huumia.
(Swahili: Kenya)

When elephants fight, the grass (reeds) get hurt.

Explanation:
Innocent people are hurt when leaders or officials are
involved in disputes.

Abofra bo envaw, na ommo akekire.
(Oji: Nigeria)

A child may crush a snail, but it cannot crush a tortoise.

Explanation:
Do not attempt to do things
that are beyond one's
strength. Do not aim for
things that are beyond
one's reach.

Ocoo mini oceeri mi ci ni.
(Lugbara: Uganda)

The dog that you have reared bites you.

Explanation:
A person one has nurtured or benefited in some way
may turn against one.

Inja Umoya.
(Xhosa: South Africa)

A dog of the wind.

Explanation:
This proverb refers to a restless person: one that
changes direction as often as the wind.

Dikgomo ke banka ya Mosotho.
(Sotho: Lesotho)

Cattle are the bank of a Mosotho.

Explanation:
A Mosotho's wealth is invested in his cattle.

Iqaqa aliziva kunuka.
(Xhosa: South Africa)

The polecat is not aware of its smell.

Explanation:
One is often blind to one's own weaknesses.

Ukuhlinza impuku.
(Xhosa: South Africa)

To skin a mouse.

Explanation:
A mouse can be skinned without anyone noticing,
but skinning a larger beast such as an ox is
highly visible. This proverb refers to any
action that is done secretly.

Hebu kiishe, huchoma mkia.
(Swahili: Kenya)

The one who waits for the whole animal to be seen, spears its tail.

Explanation:
If one is too cautious, one might lose out on an opportunity.

Yimbabala yolwantunge.
(Xhosa: South Africa)

He is a buck of an endless forest.

Explanation:
He is a restless person, never staying long in the same place.

Poo, ga di nne pedi mo sakeng.
(Tswana: Botswana)

Two bulls cannot live in the same kraal.

Explanation:
Two bulls living in the same kraal will fight each other.
This proverb is used when a decision has to be made
between two options.

Odru ni ti 'i le.
(Lugbara: Uganda)

A buffalo gives birth to one like itself.

Explanation:
In most cases, parents give their temperament and
character to their children.

Sa kogolen be dogo.
(Bambara: Mali)

The serpent that is hidden increases in size.

Explanation:
Weaknesses in ourselves get stronger if not corrected.

Akunyoka yakhohlwa ngumgodi wayo.
(Zulu: South Africa)

There is not a snake that forgets its hole.

Explanation:
No person forgets home or a place of refuge, retreating to it when life becomes difficult.

100 animals

Mbiti yi mwana ndiisaa ikamina.
(Akamba: Kenya)

The hyena with a cub does not consume all the available food.

Explanation:
Parents would rather sacrifice food for themselves than let their children go hungry.

*Ingwe ikhotha amabala ayo
amhlophe mamnyama.*
(Zulu: South Africa)

A leopard licks both its white and black spots.

Explanation:
Just as a leopard licks all its spots, justice should be
administered fairly to all by those in authority.

Ngwana a ka feta gare ga molete wa tau.
(Northern Sotho: South Africa)

A child can go through the hole of a lion.

Explanation:
Adults should be open to what children say.

*Akukho ranincwa lingagqimiyo
kowalo umxuma.*
(Xhosa: South Africa)

There is not a beast that does not roar in its own den.

Explanation:
A man is king in his own home.

A'da ku si, ozoo si fu zaramataru.
(Lugbara: Uganda)

Because of the lack of criticism, the warthog's teeth have grown disproportionately long.

Explanation:
Projects and people should welcome criticism and correction so that they do not develop incorrectly. This also refers to the timely correction of a developing child and the willingness to accept criticism.

Yakuira yuraga we kianagima.
(Kimbeere, an Embu dialect: Kenya)

A goat that is loose does not listen to the shepherd's voice.

Explanation:
A goat that roams freely, will not heed the instructions of the shepherd. Similarly, a person who is rebellious will not listen when told what to do.

Ino manga ondjupa, ongombe inayi vala.
(Ovambo: Namibia)

Do not get the churn ready for use before the cow has given birth to its calf.

Explanation:
This Ovambo proverb cautions one not to boast of one's possessions before one has acquired them.

Yehl' inkaw' emthini.
(Xhosa: South Africa)

The monkey moves down from the tree.

Explanation:
When a monkey leaves his natural habitat,
he is vulnerable to man and other predators.
This proverb refers to a person who has allowed
himself to be vulnerable.

U tla di tlhaolela di bekeroe.
(Sechuana: Botswana)

You'll remove the rams from the flock of sheep after they have already mated.

Explanation:
This proverb encourages one to think and plan ahead
and thus avoid unnecessary mistakes.

106 animals

Impungushe kayivalelwa nezimvu.
(Zulu: South Africa)

The jackal is not kept in the same kraal with the sheep.

Explanation:
As the jackal is a predator for the sheep, it would be unwise to house them together. Likewise it is foolish to put together things or people that should be kept apart.

birds

*Lapho kukhon' isidumbu,
yilapho kukhon' amanqe.*
(Zulu: South Africa)

Where there is a carcass, the vultures will be present.

Explanation:
Vultures are scavengers and when an animal dies, they quickly descend on it. This proverb is said of people who always watch for the demise of others in the hope that there will be some pickings for them.

Kila ndege huruka na mbawa zake.
(Swahili: Kenya)

Every bird flies with its own wings.

Explanation:
Every person has what it takes to live their life.

Intaka yakha ngoboya bezinye.
(Xhosa: South Africa)

A bird builds with the feathers of others.

Explanation:
No-one can be totally self-sufficient.

Aria oja 'I jo obi ku.
(Lugbara: Uganda)

A bird does not alter the way of building its nest.

Explanation:
Just as a bird is not able to change the way in which it builds its nest, it is difficult for humans to change their ingrained habits.

Inyoni kayiphumuli.
(Zulu: South Africa)

He is the bird that does not rest.

Explanation:
The cattle egret is often referred to in this way because it appears to fly long distances without resting. This proverb is used to describe a.person who does not sit still.

Kachenche kubantu kwabo dikonbo.
(Songe: Democratic Republic of Congo)

Kachenche (a tiny bird) is not important among strangers, but it is important on home ground.

Explanation:
One should not judge a person by outward appearances. One needs to take the whole person into account. The meaning is similar to 'one should not judge a book by its cover'.

Akukho nyon' endiz' ingahlali phansi.
(Zulu: South Africa)

There is not a bird that flies and never sits down.

Explanation:
Just as a bird takes a rest, one should take a break when working.

Ko se eku ko se eiye ajao.
(Yoruba: Nigeria)

The bat is neither rat nor bird.

Explanation:
A person is neither one thing nor the other.

Aria wura aluri ei nga tu alu.
(Lugbara: Uganda)

The same-coloured birds fly together.

Explanation:
Just as birds of the same species are found together,
people who are similar seek out each other. This
proverb usually refers to those people with negative
characteristics that congregate together.

Uhlekwe zinyoni.
(Zulu: South Africa)

He is laughed at by the birds.

Explanation:
This is said of a person who is on a futile mission: one
that is so irrational or unlikely to be fulfilled that even
the birds laugh at him.

Umke namangabangaba aselwandle.
(Xhosa: South Africa)

He has gone in search of the (fantastical) birds of the sea.

Explanation:
This proverb is said of someone whose dreams and
ambitions are unlikely to be fulfilled.

Ke hoole okunyangadhala, na ki ifala komukodhi omunene.
(Ovambo: Namibia)

He who likes to wander, places himself in the claws of a hawk.

Explanation:
This Ovambo proverb cautions those who wander aimlessly, as it leads to disaster.

Oidilona jomokuti ohai valua tai tondoka.
(Ovambo: Namibia)

Birds in the forest are born with the ability to run.

Explanation:
This proverb cautions one to be careful when one is in a forest.

insects

Unebhungan' ekhanda.
(Zulu: South Africa)

He has a beetle in his head.

Explanation:
This proverb is said of someone who does abnormal things and it suggests that there is something in the person's head that is producing behaviour which is different or abnormal.

Akukho mpukane inqakulela enye.
(Xhosa: South Africa)

One fly does not provide for another one.

Explanation:
Just as each fly provides for himself, this proverb encourages the idle and lazy to be more diligent and hardworking and to fend for themselves.

Emirin nje 'ni ko ti nja.
(Yoruba: Nigeria)

The sand-fly's sting is not as severe as poverty.

Explanation:
The sharp sting of the sand-fly is easier to tolerate than poverty.

Se ipelele tsie e fofa.
(Tswana: Botswana)

Do not boast of the locusts that are flying overhead.

Explanation:
This proverb cautions people against boasting of acquiring something until it is safely in the hand.

Apendaye asali huumwa na nyuki.
(Kuria: Tanzania)

Bees sting he who loves to eat honey.

Explanation:
Great success is
achieved through
difficult and painful
experiences.

Omeva ihaelinjenge ehena kapuka.
(Ovambo: Namibia)

Water does not ripple without an insect.

Explanation:
A person always has a reason for becoming angry.

Ecekelendreki drile ako si ababa.
(Lugbara: Uganda)

The black ants are in disarray because of lack of leadership.

Explanation:
When seeking food or migrating, black ants follow a leader, but when there is no leader, the ants move in all directions. Likewise, sound leaders need to be put in place and nurtured.

food
& drink

Jungu kuu halikosi ukoko.
(Swahili: East Africa)

A large cooking pot contains hard-burnt rice.

Explanation:
This proverb is used to encourage the young to be patient and to persevere until their goals in life are reached.

Abe baakon na sei ensa.
(Oji: Nigeria)

One palm tree spoils the palm wine.

Explanation:
When the wine tapped from individual palm trees is mixed, if one tree has provided bad wine, all the wine will be spoiled.

Wosen mi adidi-a, misen wo nna.
(Oji: Nigeria)

If you are superior to me in eating, I am superior to you in sleeping.

Explanation:
No one person possesses every talent. Some are better than others in some respects, but worse than others in other respects.

Atannayita: y'atenda nnyina obufumbi (=okufumba).
(Ganda: Uganda)

The person who has not travelled a great deal, thinks that his or her mother is the best cook.

Explanation:
A person who has not experienced life beyond home can become self-centred and isolated. Similarly, people who have not travelled far from home can become very provincial in their outlook on life.
This proverb is used to promote the fact that 'travel broadens the mind'.

Udla ukutya kokuhamba.
(Xhosa: South Africa)

He eats roadside food.

Explanation:
This proverb refers to an individual who is never at home to eat the food cooked at home. He eats what he can when he takes to the road.

Amvu ni 'ba anyajo ni.
(Lugbara: Uganda)

A man's field is his stomach.

Explanation:
A man's fields provide food for him. This proverb
encourages man to work in his fields or to do work in
order to survive and fulfil his needs.

Omkeli haj oondoza ji etele iikulja.
(Ovambo: Namibia)

Peace fattens more than food.

Explanation:
Peace is more beneficial than food. When there is no
peace, the people are ill at ease.

Mbaara ti ûcûrû.
(Gikuyu: Kenya)

War is not porridge.

Explanation:
Among the Gikuyu in Kenya, porridge was offered to visitors to welcome them to the home. It was also served at breakfast and all present were offered generous portions.

This proverb contrasts porridge, a healthy, wholesome option, with war that is devastating and to be avoided. It can also be used to encourage disputing parties to make peace with one another.

Amathang' ahlanzel' abangenangobo.
(Zulu: South Africa)

The pumpkins bear fruit for those who have no storage space.

Explanation:
This proverb refers to those who achieve great success in life when they are not expected to do so.

Mbajaney dou faikey dee ou borome am.
(Oji: Nigeria)

The cup does not find out that its master has died.

Explanation:
The cup does not die with its owner, as it is passed on to other hands.

Kan qabbanaauf harka/kan houf fal-aana.
(Oromo: Ethiopia)

The hand, for what is cold, the spoon for what is hot.

Explanation:
There is always a tactful or correct way to handle things.

Okhalia weng 'ene tawe.
(Bukusu: Kenya)

Do not eat on your own.

Explanation:
This proverb encourages one not to be selfish and to share one's resources with others.

Udl' ukudla kwamudla.
(Zulu: South Africa)

He ate the food that in turn ate him.

Explanation:
This proverb is used to refer to someone who has been
poisoned by food or when a pleasurable activity has
painful repercussions.

Kula kutamu, kulima mavune.
(Swahili: East Africa)

The act of eating is pleasurable, but digging makes one tired.

Explanation:
It is good to reap the fruit of one's labour after a tiresome effort.

Sejo-senyane ha se fete molomo.
(Sotho: Lesotho)

Half a loaf of bread is better than none.

Explanation:
One should be grateful for small mercies.

Agbeje ko koro ni ille nla.
(Yoruba: Nigeria)

The squash is never sour in a big family.

Explanation:
Agbeje is a pumpkin that ripens early before the other
vegetables and thus is eaten early in the season. This
proverb warns that in a home with many people, there
should not be waste.

Na yai de tes bifo moht.
(Krio: Sierra Leone)

The eye tastes before the mouth does.

Explanation:
If the food appeals to the eye, it will be eaten.

U re go bona thola borethe ka ko ntle,
mo teng e botlhoko.
(Sechuana: Botswana)

Do not be misled by the glossy appearance of a wild apple. Inside it is bitter.

Explanation:
All that glitters is not gold. Appearances are deceptive.

nature

*Okro tik nor de grow
pas en master.*
(Krio: Sierra Leone)

An okra tree will never exceed its master in height.

Explanation:
No man is greater than his master.

Umafa evuka njengenyanga.
(Xhosa: South Africa)

It dies and rises like the moon.

Explanation:
This proverb refers to an issue that keeps coming up after it has been laid to rest.

Uusiku waa nomwedhi.
(Ovambo: Namibia)

Night without moonlight.

Explanation:
The evil that is in man is exposed. Things that are hidden are revealed.

Nyaku ni 'ba piri ma andri ni.
(Lugbara: Uganda)

Earth is the mother of all.

Explanation:

Like a mother, the earth can feed everyone by the crops it produces. The only requirement is that people cultivate it.

Nalukolekejaga sonda (ng'weli) walola lwala.
(Sukuma: Tanzania)

I pointed to the stars (the moon) and all you saw was my finger-tip.

Explanation:
This Sukuma proverb refers to the fact that people can focus on the incorrect or insignificant part of the matter and miss the most important part.

Charova sei chando chakwidza hamba mumuti.
(Shona: Zimbabwe)

The frost must have been very severe to motivate the tortoise to climb the tree.

Explanation:
People are capable of doing impossible things.

Afa dri daapi vule ku ri yi ni.
(Lugbara: Uganda)

Water does not return.

Explanation:
Unlike circumstances and events that may recur again,
and people who may return after they have gone,
water does not return.

Yinkungu nelanga.
(Xhosa: South Africa)

The mist and the sun are together.

Explanation:
This proverb is used to convey a very large number.

Eno limwe kali tsakana hambo.
(Ovambo: Nambia)

One tree is not enough to build a fence.

Explanation:
One person cannot alleviate all the poverty in a country.

Kawuwelw' umful' ugcwele.
(Zulu: South Africa)

A river is not crossed when it is in flood.

Explanation:
If one tries to cross a fast-flowing river when it is in flood, one might get swept away. Similarly, one should not knowingly become involved in a dangerous situation.

Etu ece o'du ku.
(Lugbara: Uganda)

The sun rises every day.

Explanation:
Daily routines are as regular as the sun's rising.
The proverb also refers to the fact that there will be
another day tomorrow.

Nsungwi ya mtuwa sisiliridwa.
(Chewa: Malawi)

A young, tender bamboo cannot be used (for building).

Explanation:
If a man is trying to build a strong marriage, he should not go after other women at the same time. It is like using yellow bamboo shoots to build a hut. They might look good, but they are not strong enough for the structure.

This proverb is also found in the Nyanja language spoken in Mozambique, Zambia and Zimbabwe.

Unapoanika unakausha.
(Kuria: Tanzania)

It dries when it is put in the sun.

Explanation:
When one's problems are hidden, no-one else is aware
of them. When they are revealed, people are in a better
position to help.

Mukola kuzhika mambo a nsulo.
(Northern Sotho: South Africa)

A river runs deep because of its source.

Explanation:
Parents and elders should be held in high regard as
they are the source of one's life.

Iso liwel' umful' ugcwele.
(Zulu: South Africa)

The eye crosses a river that is flooded.

Explanation:
One often longs for things that are beyond one's reach.

Wonko bi afum da, wose: mi enku ni kuafo.
(Oji: Nigeria)

You might be inclined to think that you are the only planter if you never entered another man's plantation.

Explanation:
One is likely to view life only from one's own perspective.

general

Ajadi agbon odi olara.
(Yoruba: Nigeria)

A basket with a broken bottom is useless.

Explanation:
A basket that is broken cannot hold anything.
This proverb is used to describe someone who never achieves anything.

Ichaka mi che egwa.
(Igala: Nigeria)

I have ten pairs of trousers.

Explanation:
One is only able to wear one pair of trousers at a time.
Therefore this proverb cautions against having
too many material possessions as they
require maintenance.

Andi ni nya muzu.
(Lugbara: Uganda)

The foreigner eats in order to go.

Explanation:
A stranger may enjoy the hospitality of those with
whom he is staying, but sooner or later he will leave as
his home is elsewhere. Therefore one cannot depend
on a stranger or foreigner.

Ditlamelo tsa pula di baakangoa gale.
(Tswana: Botswana)

One needs to take precautions against rain before it falls.

Explanation:
Put up your sail when the weather is fair.

U tla kgadisa mocoetsana.
(Tswana: Botswana)

You will drain the fountain until it dries.

Explanation:
This proverb cautions people not to abuse
another's kindness.

Agbassa babba okuta.
(Yoruba: Nigeria)

A boulder is the father of rocks.

Explanation:
This proverb is used to compliment, flatter or refer to a person who is head and shoulders above the rest.

Ompitula kayi man'ondombe.
(Ovambo: Namibia)

The one who passes by does not drain the pond.

Explanation:
A guest does not eat all the food that is in the home.

Bogosi boa tsaleloa, ga bo loeloe.
(Tswana: Botswana)

A person should be born for the role of king, not fight for it.

Explanation:
A king is born, not created. Natural leaders are born with leadership qualities.

Ucel' amehlo.
(Xhosa: South Africa)

He or she is asking for eyes.

Explanation:
This proverb is used when someone is seeking
attention for themselves.

Iyak okpun onyon aka idim.
(Efik: Nigeria)

When grown, the fish returns to his little river.

Explanation:
This proverb cautions those who have improved themselves not to forget their origins.

Nima iha kalele uulamba waa nomeya.
(Ovambo: Namibia)

Man does not stay at holes that are waterless.

Explanation:
Man does not stay at a place where there is nothing on offer.

Aco ni 'i 'dipi 'i.
(Lugbara: Uganda)

The hoe is only familiar with its owner.

Explanation:
The close relationship between the hoe and its owner should not be interfered with. The implication is that the hoe would not work as well in the hands of another. This proverb is used to warn others against borrowing or lending personal possessions.

Darbatani jinfu hinqabatani.
(Oromo: Ethiopia)

After you have thrown the spear, you cannot catch hold of its end.

Explanation:
Once something is done one cannot undo it, though one may regret having done it.

Mgeni njoo, mwenyeji apone.
(Swahili: Eastern and Central Africa)

Let the guest come so that the host or hostess may benefit (get well).

Explanation:
The visitor brings blessings to the home
and the people living there.
Such blessings may be in the form of meat or bananas
in an attempt to foster good relations with the
household. The arrival of the guest also signifies a
celebratory meal (for which a chicken or goat may be
slaughtered) and all the family members will benefit as
a result of the visit.
The guest may also bring news of friends or
relatives living in other parts of the country.
Sometimes the guest also brings new medicine
to help those who are sick.
This proverb is also found in the Haya language
(Tanzania) and Luyia (Kenya).